CHARACTERS

Major Characters: four females, three males

    CINDERELLA
    MELBA
    GOLDILOCKS
    RED RIDING HOOD

    PRINCE CHARMING
    JASON
    A.E. RUMPLESTILSKIN

Minor Characters: seven females, three males

    PRINCESS 1
    PRINCESS 2
    PRINCESS 3
    RAPUNZEL
    GRETCHEN
    ALETTA
    NANINE

    PIED PIPER
    JACK CALDWELL
    VOICE OF NARRATOR/MIRROR

SET

The play is set in the Royal Castle in the Enchanted Kingdom. It may be presented with a suggested set. Act I is a bedroom, Acts II and III are the royal ball-room. The addition/removal of a bed is all that is required to change the set. More ambitious designs may be utilized, of course.

3

DESCRIPTION OF CHARACTERS

CINDERELLA, a charming woman in her early forties. In Scene I she wears nightclothes which she changes for a royal robe suited to a fairy-tale queen. For the royal ball she adds additional adornment.

PRINCE CHARMING, king of the Enchanted Kingdom, in his mid-forties, a little chubby, a little bald. He begins Scene I in a long nightshirt, changes to royal garments suited to a fairy-tale king.

MELBA, Cinderella's fairy godmother, a boisterous, pushy woman in her early sixties. She wears levis, a blue jean jacket, a cowboy hat, a lasso on her belt, and guns in holsters.

GOLDILOCKS, a lovely young girl 18 or 20 with long gold curls. She wears a long gown.

RED RIDING HOOD, a slinky, sultry beauty in her twenties. She is dressed in a tightfitting red gown and red cape lined in white fur.

JASON, a sweet, well-intentioned bumbler in his twenties who has one arm and one swan's wing. He wears clothing suited to a fairy-tale adviser to the king.

A.E. RUMPLESTILSKIN, a quarrelsome, whiney old man, in his mid-fifties. He wears more common garments than the royal group.

PIED PIPER, a young man in his twenties. He is dressed in clothing suitable to a fairy-tale piper.

JACK CALDWELL, of bean stalk fame, in his twenties. He is dressed to attend the royal ball.

Happily Ever

Once Upon

A FAIRY TALE PARODY
IN THREE ACTS

by Virginia Kidd

SAMUEL FRENCH, INC.

25 WEST 45TH STREET   NEW YORK 10036
7623 SUNSET BOULEVARD   HOLLYWOOD 90046
LONDON   *TORONTO*

4 6 5 3 2 1 9 4 1

RAPUNZEL, a young woman in her twenties, rather snobbish, with hair so long it drags the floor. She is dressed to attend the ball.

PRINCESS 1
PRINCESS 2
PRINCESS 3
GRETCHEN
ALETTA
NANINE

} Guests at the royal ball. All are in their twenties and wear clothing suited to a ball in the Enchanted Kingdom.

Happily Ever Once Upon

ACT I

House lights fade and VOICE OF NARRATOR *begins even
before the curtain rises. In the middle of* NAR-
RATOR'S *speech, the curtain slowly lifts to reveal
the magical world of the Enchanted Kingdom,
to be more specific, the bedroom of the castle of*
PRINCE CHARMING *and his lovely wife* CINDERELLA.
*We hear angelic soprano voices (which we rec-
ognize instantly as enchanted harps) singing
gentle melodies a la Walt Disney, and from some
unseen source soft glitter seems to be falling.*

VOICE OF NARRATOR. Once upon a time, in a far away
land called the Enchanted Kingdom lived a handsome
prince and his charming wife. The royal couple met at
a village ball where the lovely queen lost a glass
slipper. Rumors at the time suggested a third party
was involved in the acquisition of the slippers, but the
question went unsettled and the rumors died down.
Not knowing the name of his love, the prince tried the
slipper on every woman in the royal kingdom until
he found his bride. And they were married in a gala
celebration and settled down in the royal castle where
they lived happily ever after.

*(The golden voices rise in majestic beauty, but the
moment is shattered by the brash ringing of a
terribly vocal alarm clock. The singing ceases
abruptly as do the glitter and other magical
effects. We hear only the* PRINCE.)

PRINCE. Damn! Damn! Damn! Damn! Damn!

CINDERELLA. It's your turn.

PRINCE. Damn foreign inventions. Where are the servants?

(CINDERELLA *sits up. She was once a famed beauty, and even now in her forties she is attractive. She is more attractive, of course, when her hair is not up in rollers as it is now and when her face is not covered with night cream. She begins to do sit ups.*)

CINDERELLA. Most of them quit.

PRINCE. Quit Prince Charming?

CINDERELLA. For financial reasons.

PRINCE. Just what do you mean by that? (PRINCE *is now sitting up. He wears a long gown and a night cap beneath which is a balding head. Despite his increasingly expanding tummy we can see that here, too, is a person who once cut a fine figure.*)

CINDERELLA. Just what you think. (*Counting sit ups.*) Seven. They haven't been paid in months.

PRINCE. And why not, may I ask?

CINDERELLA. Eight. Oh, Charm, come on, it's me. Nine. You don't have to put on a show for me. We're busted. Ten.

PRINCE. Cinderella! I will not allow that kind of talk—

CINDERELLA. Are you gonna get the alarm or am I?

PRINCE. Well, I'm not! I do not get alarms. I am his royal imperial majesty, Holy Ruler of the Enchanted Empire, Keeper of the Faith, Defender—

CINDERELLA. (*Throwing covers aside and rising.*) —of the Undertrod, Protector of Justice, etc., etc., etc. I'll get it. I am Cinderella, Sitter by Fireplaces, Queen Consort, and General Alarm Stopper. (*She stops alarm.*) It is spending money on foreign inventions like this that is putting us in the poor house.

PRINCE. There are no poor houses in the Enchanted Kingdom.

CINDERELLA. The poor castle then. (*She begins to fix her hair.* PRINCE *rises and begins dressing through the scene until the entrance of* JASON, *when he is fully dressed.*)

PRINCE. When my father was alive, there was money in the Royal Till. There was always money for balls, parties, uniforms, shining white knight costumes complete with horse. What happened to it all?

CINDERELLA. Charm, that was twenty years ago. Twenty years. For all that time we've been spending money like it was water and bringing none in, and there's inflation and devaluation of the ducat and export imbalances—

PRINCE. Twenty years ago was when I married you. That's when the money started to go.

CINDERELLA. So now it's my fault?

PRINCE. I didn't say it was your fault. But it is an amazing coincidence, that's all.

CINDERELLA. The only coincidence is that after you married me the kids started coming. That's the dollar drain, right there! You're the one who insisted that Junior "must go to the finest schools."

PRINCE. He's going to be king of the realm someday. He must learn how to carry himself, how to be noble, kind, holy, Defender of the Undertrod, Upholder of—

CINDERELLA. I'm sorry I brought it up.

PRINCE. But you did bring it up! He has learned the important things in life at that school—

CINDERELLA. All he's learned is how to kiss sleeping princesses and it seems to me he'd learned that already from practicing on the maids, so why waste money on Prince School?

PRINCE. But, my dear, those are the maids who are still with us! That's a point to consider. (*Pause.*) As long as we are talking about expenses, there is the slight matter of your relations.

CINDERELLA. Oh, Charm, what can you do about relations? I admit they cost a lot—

PRINCE. A lot? Your godmother alone is personally responsible for the export-import imbalance. Every farthing she gets she unloads in America making Grade B western movies.

CINDERELLA. But, Darling, when you have a talent, you simply—

PRINCE. Talent? Her top selling movie, Cindy, her top movie grossed $18. $18! I don't understand why you keep shelling it out. You'd think she had some kind of hold over you.

CINDERELLA. (*Quickly.*) Why do you say that?

PRINCE. Because you're so completely unreasonable about it. And she's only one. What about Snow White?

CINDERELLA. Well, surely you can't object to her. That poor girl was in dreadful health. She'd been poisoned, left out lying in the forest for months. It's no wonder she was so upset.

PRINCE. She was upset because she gave up seven men for one—

CINDERELLA. Don't you say that! Don't you say that about my cousin! Those little men were like fathers to her, nothing more!

PRINCE. Oh, yes, fathers, tell me about it.

CINDERELLA. Now, Charming, I'm getting angry! Her father and mine were brothers, very close. Snow had a terrible life. She was raised by a horrible wicked woman, she was treated mercilessly. (*Sniffs.*) *I* can understand something like that.

PRINCE. (*Here-we-go-again reaction.*) Ohhhhh.

CINDERELLA. Well, if you had ever been mistreated, if you had known anything beyond this plushy life—

PRINCE. All right! All right! She had a miserable childhood. She's warped for life. I'll buy it. (CINDERELLA *sniffs.*) Not to mention the gay old times she had in the woods.

CINDERELLA. Charm! (*He laughs, she throws a pillow*

*at him, he ducks, grabs her; she struggles weakly, with
little effort; he kisses her; she returns the kiss.*)

PRINCE. (*Teasing.*) Poor little Cinderelly had to
clean the fireplace, oh, poor Cinderelly.

CINDERELLA. (*Struggling to push away.*) You make
me so mad! You just—

PRINCE. (*Kissing her again.*) It was a long time ago,
little scrub girl. (*He returns to his dressing.*) Besides,
you weren't treated too badly. You sure didn't come
to the ball in rags tromping through the mud on foot,
did you?

CINDERELLA. (*Carefully.*) That was—another matter.

PRINCE. What kind of matter?

CINDERELLA. My godmother helped me. That's why
I've been so grateful to her.

PRINCE. All of which has very little to do with this
girl who's coming today.

CINDERELLA. Goldilocks.

PRINCE. Your family have the weirdest names.

CINDERELLA. I don't think it's asking too much in the
name of family to help those who have been less fortu-
nate than we. I know if what happened to Goldie happened to one of our little girls—

PRINCE. Our little girls are all big girls now.

CINDERELLA. Alanis is only eleven!

PRINCE. Well, Aletha is eighteen and a sillier girl
I've never seen. Do you know what she wanted to do
yesterday? Bring a frog to the table. A frog! She said
she was in love with him. I squashed him flatter than
the rug! I don't understand our children.

CINDERELLA. Well, the little ones are sweet, dear; it's
only the big ones that are so confusing.

PRINCE. The little ones are the worst! I don't think
Peter's ever going to grow up. He claims he's learning
to fly. He goes around clutching that little brown
pouch, claims he's got a fairy locked up in there.

When I was his age, I didn't even know a word like that.

CINDERELLA. It's Midas I worry about. Never have I see a greater materialist. I think he'd be happy if everything he touched turned to gold. I said, do you want the lovely roses to turn to gold, do you want a gold sky around you, do you want your own Momie to be gold, and, Charm! there was such a gleam in his eye as he looked at me I was frightened.

PRINCE. Don't worry about the boys. When they're old enough, I'll send them off on some task. Bring me a princess in a nut or something. I'll get Jason to advise them.

CINDERELLA. (*Sarcastically.*) Yes, let Jason do it.

PRINCE. (*Defensively.*) Jason is my loyal confidant and economic adviser!

CINDERELLA. Jason is a dear, kind, well meaning man, but he is also a bumbling idiot.

PRINCE. You make fun of Jason, but you know he's the most loyal of my servants! He's never even hinted of leaving when all others have walked out on me in my hour of need.

CINDERELLA. Jason has faithfully remained with you because who else would hire a man with one arm and one swan's wing.

PRINCE. You know his recommendations for our economic plight have been of the highest order—except for that one little slip.

CINDERELLA. What one little slip?

PRINCE. He wanted to give tours of the Enchanted Kingdom. Just like owners of British castles. I said, never! Never would I allow strangers to wander through my kingdom ridiculing, pointing at things. We don't need money that badly. He was quite chagrined. I was a little hard on him, I guess. He meant well.

CINDERELLA. He always means well! He meant well when we complained about the obstructions to the

view and he cut down that bean stalk and left Jack
Caldwell stranded in the sky for three days while
another stalk grew. That little law suit took 28,000
ducats out of court. Damages to a magic, not plain,
but magic bean stalk, plus fear and mental anguish
for Jack. Not to mention the impact on the bean
market.

PRINCE. Yes, but this time Jason's really on to
something, Cindy. Our financial troubles will be a
thing of the past. (*He pulls bell cord.*)

CINDERELLA. The bell doesn't work.

PRINCE. Why not?

CINDERELLA. The loyal and patriotic electric com-
pany wants its bill paid.

PRINCE. (*Crosses to door, calls out.*) Jason! Jason!

CINDERELLA. So tell me the grandiose scheme.

PRINCE. It's not a scheme. It's a man.

CINDERELLA. A man?

PRINCE. A tiny little man, Cindy, he— (*Looks
around, comes close as though it is a secret.*) —he
spins gold from straw!

CINDERELLA. Oh, Charm! Jason's done it to you
again!

PRINCE. No, he really does! It's true. Our vaults
will be filled again in no time!

(JASON *enters.* JASON *is a handsome young man in his
mid-twenties who has every aspect of being a
Prince Charming himself except for the unfortunate swan's wing which replaces his right arm
and the equally unfortunate habit he has of
somehow virtually annihilating every venture
with which he is associated.*)

JASON. Did you send for me, your Majesty? (*He
bows, sweeping his hat behind him, knocking crystal
knick knacks from the table helter skelter.*)

CINDERELLA. He sent for you. He wants to do a

scientific study to see how much destruction one single human being can accomplish in any given five minute period.

JASON. I'm terribly sorry, your Highness.

CINDERELLA. Always, Jason. You always are.

PRINCE. Tell us about the venture, Jason. How goes it?

JASON. What?

PRINCE. The venture.

JASON. What venture?

PRINCE. The little man, the little man!

JASON. Oh, that venture! The little man!

PRINCE. Yes.

JASON. The one we're looking for.

PRINCE. Yes, the one we're looking for.

JASON. (*Proudly.*) Well, we're looking for him.

PRINCE. Oh. Well, good, good. Think we'll find him?

JASON. (*Still caught up in his pride.*) Oh, no, not a chance.

PRINCE. (*Bellowing.*) What do you mean, not a chance? (*He backs* JASON *against the window.* JASON'S *sword catches in the curtain.*)

JASON. (*Squeaking.*) Well, your majesty, sir, we don't know his name.

PRINCE. Don't know his name?

JASON. No, sir.

PRINCE. What does that have to do with it?

JASON. Well, how can you find somebody if you don't know his name? You can't even look in the directory.

CINDERELLA. Look in the yellow pages under Little Men.

JASON. We could try Gold Spinners.

PRINCE. (*Storming from window.*) Oh, Jason! Come! It can't be that hard to find out who he is.

JASON. (*Following* PRINCE.) It has been said, sir, that her majesty is very intuitive about such— (*As*

JASON *moves from wall, the curtains are pulled down.*)
Terribly sorry.

CINDERELLA. It was to be expected.

JASON. (*Disentangling sword.*) I was about to say,
sir, that her majesty might could suggest a name we
could investigate. (*They stare at her.*)

CINDERELLA. Smith, John.

JASON. Oh, thank you, your Queeness. I'll just write
it down. I just stuck my quill in here somewhere.
(*Looks through pockets.*) Oh, I guess I put it here.
(*Indicates swan wing.*) Oh, I shouldn't have. Well,
I'll just get another. (*They watch him, fascinated.*)
Oh, eeny, meeny, minny, moe. This one. Ha, ha. I'll
just pull it out. (*Pause.*) It's gonna hurt. (*No re-
sponse.*) Well, I'll do it. For the kingdom. (*Pulls
feather out of arm.*) Oh! Oh! Ohhhhhh! That smarts!
I'll need something to write on.

CINDERELLA. Definitely.

JASON. Well, here in my pocket. A letter. I'll write
on that. Now. Ink. Uh—ink?

CINDERELLA. No ink.

PRINCE. No ink.

JASON. Oh. Well, I'll just go downstairs— (*He
turns, bumps end table.*) Oh, uh—ha, ha.

CINDERELLA. Ha, ha.

JASON. (*Looking at letter.*) Oh! Oh, by the way,
ha, ha, this letter is for you. Came last week. I meant
to bring it before— (*He walks to* CINDERELLA, *trips
on rug, falls into her, knocking her over.*) Terribly
sorry.

CINDERELLA. You always are, Jason.

JASON. I'm really just—a bumbler. I know it. Go
ahead and say it.

CINDERELLA. Would you get off me first?

JASON. Oh, terribly sorry. (*He kneels on her hand
as he gets up.*)

CINDERELLA. Jason!

JASON. Oh, sorry. (*They get up.*)

CINDERELLA. (*Taking letter.*) Thank you. (*She reads as* PRINCE *sits* JASON *in a chair.*)

PRINCE. Don't move.

JASON. It's my swan wing. It throws me off balance. I haven't always had it, you know.

CINDERELLA. Darling, it's from Goldie. She's arriving today and she's bringing a friend. Oh, that'll be nice. That'll be an extra girl at the ball.

PRINCE. What ball?

CINDERELLA. Didn't we mention the ball?

PRINCE. No, you didn't mention the ball.

CINDERELLA. Jason, didn't you mention the ball?

JASON. Oh, I'm sure we mentioned the ball, sir. (*He starts to rise.*)

PRINCE. (*To* JASON.) Don't get up.

CINDERELLA. Well, it's next week. In Goldie's honor. To sort of introduce her around.

PRINCE. Introduce her around—how long is she going to be here?

CINDERELLA. Well, Darling, for a while. She-she needs to get to know people. She—well—she needs to get to know some young men. She's terribly repressed, Darling.

PRINCE. So am I going to be when we go broke.

CINDERELLA. Well, going broke is quite different from what happened to her. (*Sniffs.*) Poor child.

PRINCE. All right, how many little men took care of her?

CINDERELLA. It wasn't men, it was bears!

PRINCE. Bears?

CINDERELLA. She was almost eaten, poor child. Returned home disheveled and in hysterics. She was under doctors care for—well, years. And she's terribly frightened of people now they say.

PRINCE. So let her go be a hermit. What's she doing bringing a friend?

CINDERELLA. Well, it's the girl who found her. When

she was wandering through the woods, lost and in hysterics, dishev—

PRINCE. All right! All right!

CINDERELLA. Besides, it won't hurt us to have a ball around her now and then. It's been a long time.

PRINCE. And whom do you have selected to lay at the altar of our little Goldilocks?

CINDERELLA. Well, of course I haven't seen her myself in years. Her mother and my mother were second cousins by marriage, but I personally don't really know Goldie, you know, intimately. But I thought in terms of Pied Piper.

JASON. Pied Piper? Oh, no! (*Rises.*)

PRINCE. (*To* JASON.) Down. (JASON *sits.*) Why Pied?

CINDERELLA. Well, it was just a thought. He's a pleasant enough fellow and still young. And besides, there just aren't that many eligible young men around these days. Prince Danton has been turned into a beast, and poor Tom Thumb, while being simply delightful and extremely well travelled, is none-the-less so terribly short, and Jack Caldwell simply reeks of the bean cannery, and why do you say, "Oh, no"?

JASON. Well, it's just that—things follow him around.

PRINCE. Things?

JASON. Animals and children and butterflies and things. (*Clutching his wing.*) Cats.

PRINCE. Well, maybe Goldie will too. When are they coming?

CINDERELLA. About thirty minutes ago. I do wish you'd go look for them.

JASON. We'll send out the army! (*He stands.*)

PRINCE. The army is on a more important mission. We'll go ourselves. Come along. (JASON'S *sleeve catches in chair, pulls chair over, rips sleeve.*)

CINDERELLA. (*To* PRINCE.) Good luck. Maybe you'd better wear your armor. (*Glances at* JASON.)

JASON. We shall return! (*He bumps into door, exits.*)

PRINCE. (*Kisses* CINDERELLA *tenderly.*) Jason means well. We'll bring your friends back. You be a good queen. (*He crosses to exit.*) If you get time, clean out the fireplace will you? (*He ducks as she throws a pillow. Laughing, he exits.* CINDERELLA *is now alone on the stage. She steps toward a screen to add jewelery, etc. to her costume, but stops as she reaches a mirror. She hesitates, looks around guiltily.*)

CINDERELLA. Mirror, mirror on the wall—

VOICE OF MIRROR. Forget it!

CINDERELLA. (*Dejected.*) A fine friend you are!

MELBA. (*Off stage.*) And a fine friend you are, too.

CINDERELLA. (*Turns, gasps.*) Melba!

(MELBA *appears in a cloud of smoke. She is in her sixties, a little overweight, but quite dolled up. She carries a magic wand and wears levis and a blue jean jacket.*)

MELBA. Hiya, Tenderfoot!

CINDERELLA. Oh, Melba.

MELBA. What is this "Oh, Melba" routine. Aren't you glad to see your old godmother?

CINDERELLA. (*After a moment she gives* MELBA *a sincere hug.*) Oh, yes I am, Melba, I am, my dear. But if you've come for money—

MELBA. Critics blasted my last movie! Said it was worse than the one before. Can't understand 'em. No taste. Lost everything you gave me.

CINDERELLA. Oh, Melba, I'm simply drained. Prince Charming doesn't have any idea how much I've given you. If he knew—

MELBA. There's a lotta things he could know.

CINDERELLA. (*Frightened.*) Melba—

MELBA. But he don't! Yeehaw! (*She throws her lasso at a chair, but misses.*) Dang it. Did that in the movie, too. Get ready, gal, we got some broncos to rope in treasury. Yeehaw!

CINDERELLA. (*She sighs, resumes putting on jewelry, makeup.*) Melba, it won't work anymore. I don't care what you say. I'm sorry you're in need. I don't have it. I don't have anything.

MELBA. That's what you always say.

CINDERELLA. But this time it's true. It's always true, but this time it's especially true.

MELBA. (*Quick drawing; her gun sticks.*) Heard you was havin' a shindig, mam. I figure anybody who can throw a shindig—

CINDERELLA. You ordered that yourself and you know it! And I seriously doubt if we can pay for it. We're getting all our supplies on credit! And it's your fault, Melba!

MELBA. Owed a favor to Goldie's godma. She backed the original version of *Melba Versus One-Eyed Pete.* Shot him dead center in the first scene.

CINDERELLA. Then what happened in the rest of the movie?

MELBA. That's when I shot the director and the cameraman.

CINDERELLA. Oh, Melba, why don't you give up? You were so good at changing pumpkins.

MELBA. Not my field. No challenge. This is exhilerating. And I'm gonna make it, baby, wait and see. I'll owe it all to you.

CINDERELLA. You can say that again! Those girls are going to be here any minute, the servants have all quit for lack of pay, I can't afford to have this ball at all. And what we do have Jason keeps breaking. Melba, I can't—

MELBA. (*Concerned.*) Hey, hey—

CINDERELLA. (*Collapsing in* MELBA'S *arms, crying.*) Oh, Melba, we just can't do it! We just can't!

MELBA. Hey, now. Come on. I didn't come here to get you all upset.

CINDERELLA. Well, you came here to take the rest of the money! Melba, there is no more!

MELBA. Now you turn around here and straighten up! Melba can take care of these things.

CINDERELLA. Then why haven't you before?

MELBA. Because it's a lot of work, that's why. You think you just say poof and it's done? It takes a lot out of a woman.

CINDERELLA. (*Hopeful.*) Melba, can you make money?

MELBA. No, I can't make money. But I can finagle things. Yeeehaw! But first—a little agreement—between you and me.

CINDERELLA. Sometimes I wish I'd never had your help.

MELBA. Oh, come now, baby, you know you love me. You know how much I'd hate to tell Prince Charming our little secret.

CINDERELLA. (*With despair.*) But you'd do it.

MELBA. Well, us fairy godmothers got to make a living somehow.

CINDERELLA. Don't you have some other lucky princesses you can blackmail?

MELBA. Oh, child, your language! I just help you remember your filial obligations, that's all. Now, let's talk no more about it. I'm sure whatever money I can arrange for the Prince to get, you will pass over to me, shall we say—fifty-fifty.

CINDERELLA. Melba!

MELBA. Well, I'm doing all the work!

CINDERELLA. (*Thoughtfully.*) Yes, you are. Why—why do you bother with us at all as intermediaries? Why don't you get your own money?

MELBA. No need to talk about that now, doggies, onward to the showdown—

CINDERELLA. Yes, there is a need to talk about it now! Why can't you get your own money?

MELBA. Very old rule of the godmother hierarchy.

Pointless. Antiquated. Established years ago when there was no need for money in—

CINDERELLA. Money is against the godmother laws! What if I turned you in?

MELBA. They'd take away a few powers and I wouldn't be able to help you as much, but I'd still have enough to turn you back into the ugly little chambermaid you were when I found you! Prince Charming would love warts on your fingers, wouldn't he, baby?

CINDERELLA. (*Fearfully.*) Melba!

MELBA. And the little pox marks on your face. The life of a scullery maid just didn't agree with you, did it?

CINDERELLA. (*Recoiling.*) You are a witch!

MELBA. Course you can't blame the maid work for your buck teeth or those wavering wall eyes, can you? Oh, we changed more than the costume that night, didn't we?

CINDERELLA. I hate you when you are like this!

MELBA. You want me to change you back and get out of your life, huh? Huh? Do you?

CINDERELLA. Melba, why do you do this to me? Why? I've always loved you.

MELBA. Except when I'm like this.

CINDERELLA. Well, why should I at times like this?

MELBA. Well—you shouldn't, mam. I just want you to remember who's in charge here. Now I need to acquire financing from—shall we say—a private source. And you're it. Now. Let us face the problems as they appear. First, you mentioned the "girls" would be here soon. Who's that?

CINDERELLA. The girls you sent. Goldilocks and Red Riding Hood.

MELBA. (*Suddenly alert.*) Red Riding Hood?

CINDERELLA. Yes. Red Riding Hood.

MELBA. I didn't send Red Riding Hood.

CINDERELLA. Well, it was in the letter. Goldie's bringing her friend Red Riding Hood.

MELBA. (*Thoughtfully.*) Now we're in for it.

CINDERELLA. Why? What's wrong with her?

MELBA. Nothing. Nothing's wrong with her. That's the first half of the problem. The second half is that being so nearly perfect she hires herself out to get close to people.

CINDERELLA. What does that mean?

MELBA. I think she's a spy.

CINDERELLA. A spy? From where?

MELBA. The Godmother Council. They're onto me. I'll have to cool it about helping you get money. You get it! (*Threateningly.*) And get it fast so I can get out of here! (*There is a knock on the door.*)

JASON. (*Outside.*) Your majesty?

CINDERELLA. Come in.

(JASON *and* GOLDIE *enter.* GOLDIE *is a lovely young woman with long golden curls and a ringing laugh. She rushes to* CINDERELLA *and hugs her.*)

GOLDIE. Oh, Aunt Cinderella, it's so good to be here. I'm so happy to see you!

CINDERELLA. Goldie! Let me look at you. Why, how you've grown! You're a young lady.

GOLDIE. Oh, Aunt Cindy, you're more beautiful then all the stories I've heard about you.

MELBA. Like magic, isn't it?

CINDERELLA. But you are the lovely one here, Goldie. Isn't she, Jason?

JASON. Yes, she is. (*He stares at her and they smile a long, intimate smile.* CINDERELLA *gasps.*)

CINDERELLA. No!

GOLDIE. What?

CINDERELLA. (*Clutching her arm as she inarticulately describes* JASON.) He's got—he—he's—

JASON. (*Still staring at* GOLDIE.) Yes, she is very

lovely. (*He spreads his wing and knocks over a lamp.*)
   CINDERELLA. Jason, damn it!

(*They clamor to pick up the lamp, but at this moment*
   PRINCE CHARMING *enters with* RED RIDING HOOD
   *on his arm. She is a sleek, slinky beauty. We
   can almost hear "The Stripper" playing in the
   background. Her red dress has been molded on
   her and her red cape and hood is lined in white
   fur. She never lets go of the* PRINCE'S *arm, and
   when she speaks we envision steam on the windows from her breathy, sultry voice.*)

   PRINCE. Uh, hi there all. Dear—uh—Cin—Cinder-
ella, I want you to meet— (*He pauses, looks at* RED
RIDING HOOD, *swims in her eyes.*) —Red Riding Hood.
   RED. Hi there.
   CINDERELLA. (*Numbly.*) Hi.
   RED. I've just been looking at your lovely castle.
I'm going to get the Princy-Wincy to show me every
—little—nook—and cranny . Ummmm. (*Smiles at
him.*) Your king is so big—and—strong. I love that
kind of man.
   CINDERELLA. Oh. Well—uh—
   RED. (*To* MELBA.) And you must be the godmother
I've heard so much about. I'm sure we'll enjoy talk-
ing, don't you think? Oh, I know I'm going to enjoy
my stay. I just know my visit is going to be terribly
interesting. Just terribly exciting. Don't you think?
   CINDERELLA. You bet. I can just hardly wait.

(*Curtain.*)

ACT II

Scene 1

TIME: One week later, morning.

SCENE: *The royal ballroom, prepared for the ball. A small table has been set downstage center where* CINDERELLA *and* MELBA *are having coffee. As the curtain rises we hear* MELBA'S *ringing voice, drawing out the first word.*

MELBA. Rum—ple—stil—skin! A.E. Rumplestilskin, Jr.! He's the one! Absolutely! Took me to the Junior Godparent Prom just before he was kicked out of the Academy for fraud. The very one.

CINDERELLA. A.E. Rumplestilskin, Jr.?

MELBA. The very one. And you say he's still going around claiming to make gold from straw?

CINDERELLA. Oh, I don't know if he's claiming it or not. It's one of Jason's schemes so heaven only knows—

MELBA. A.E. Rumplestilskin, Jr. Haven't thought of him in years. Last I heard of him he was involved in some attempted kidnapping charge—claimed the Queen of Euphoria promised him her baby.

CINDERELLA. He's a kidnapper?

MELBA. Well, there was no trial, you know. They accused him and he threw a fit right in court. Broke his foot, they say.

CINDERELLA. Melba, can he do it?

MELBA. Throw a fit? Baby, you never seen one like it. When I wouldn't kiss him goodnight—

CINDERELLA. Spin gold from straw.

24

MELBA. Oh. That I don't know. I sincerely doubt it. He always was a quack. (*Idea.*) Maybe there's a way I could help him if we got him here. But we'd have to be careful with Red around. Very careful.

CINDERELLA. Well, it's worth a try. I'll send a messenger out to Charming to tell him the name.

MELBA. No need for that. (*She stretches out her arm.*) Zot! Now he knows. (*She settles back with her cup of coffee.*) So what else is new?

CINDERELLA. Not much. There's a new swan in the pond. Beautiful creature. Simply flew in. Reminds me a little of that ugly little duckling that used to live here.

MELBA. Flew in, eh? Over the little brick outhouse?

CINDERELLA. (*Sighs.*) Oh, that.

MELBA. Oh, what?

CINDERELLA. Jason has decided all our pigs need brick stys "to keep away evil biting and ripping animals" he claims, clutching his little feathered arm. Melba, is there nothing you can do about that?

MELBA. One enchanter cannot undo the work of another enchanter. I presume he's enchanted. If he was born that way, someone must have had a lot of explaining to do!

CINDERELLA. Melba! How crude! (GOLDIE *and* RED *enter.*)

GOLDIE. Good morning, Aunt Cinderella. Queen Melba.

CINDERELLA. (*To* MELBA.) *Queen* Melba?

MELBA. Well, you gotta tell a kid something. What's she supposed to call me? Old Melba over there. Hey, you in the boots.

CINDERELLA. Good morning, girls. I hope you're rested for the ball tonight. Did you sleep well?

GOLDIE. Yes, thank you.

CINDERELLA. And you, Red?

RED. Well . . .

CINDERELLA. Yes?

RED. Well, I don't wish to complain after your and especially his Majesty's warm hospitality—

CINDERELLA. Good.

RED. But—well, I must say, I asked his highness to bring me extra mattresses. My bed had a lump in it.

CINDERELLA. A lump?

RED. That sweet man was up all night just coming in and out of my bedroom bringing mattresses for me. I must have had twenty of them and twenty soft covers. But I simply couldn't get comfortable. I feel just worn out this morning.

CINDERELLA. I'm so sorry. By the way, tarts are on the buffet. Help yourself. (GOLDIE *and* RED *cross to buffet. To* MELBA.) She feels worn out.

MELBA. Pity-full, ain't it?

CINDERELLA. Did you have anything to do with that?

MELBA. Me?

CINDERELLA. Oh, Melba, did you pull that old "pea in the bed" routine again?

MELBA. Peas are for princesses. For her it took a chamber pot!

CINDERELLA. Melba!

MELBA. (*To* GOLDIE *and* RED.) Have all the tarts you want, girls, but watch that big pie. It's full of blackbirds for some ungodly reason.

CINDERELLA. Jason thinks it will be clever to open it at the ball and let them fly out.

MELBA. Jason is a rare bird. (*Delighted with herself.*) A rare bird! Ha! I made a joke! (CINDERELLA *winces at the joke.* GOLDIE *and* RED *join them at the table.*)

CINDERELLA. Goldie, tell me, what do think of Pied? Or is it personal perhaps, hopefully?

GOLDIE. (*Hesitantly.*) He's very nice.

CINDERELLA. Yes he is. Coffee?

GOLDIE. Thank you. And he's very—well, attractive.

CINDERELLA. Oh, do you think so?

GOLDIE. He attracts all kinds of—people and—things.

CINDERELLA. Yes?

GOLDIE. I mean, children follow him around, and, and—

MELBA. Rabbits.

GOLDIE. Yes, rabbits follow him around.

MELBA. And bats.

CINDERELLA. Melba!

MELBA. Vampire bats.

GOLDIE. Everything. Bats, cats—

MELBA. Lizards, orangutans, Siberian elk, whooping cranes—

CINDERELLA. Melba—

GOLDIE. We've never been alone. Yesterday he came by boat on the river and there were fish flapping along behind him.

CINDERELLA. I'll admit Pied is much beloved by the local citizenry—

(*Just at this moment the door flies open and* PIED PIPER *crashes in, flattens himself against the wall, and slams the door shut. He is a rather ordinary young fellow whose central obsession in life is being alone in a room without animals or children.*)

GOLDIE. Pied!

PIED. Did it! Did it! Kept 'em all out! Walked along casually like I was doing nothin' special, last ten yards sprinted like hell was after me. Kept 'em out. Did it! Hiya, Goldie, Red, you Majesties.

RED. Hello there.

CINDERELLA. I understand you and Goldie are going for a stroll, Pied.

PIED. Yeah, we and all the children in the village

and thousands of wild beasts. Would you like to join us, Miss Hood?

RED. That would be lovely, I'm sure. I'll bet you know a lot about what goes on in this kingdom having the villagers around you all the time. We can chat as we walk. I just love to know all about places I visit, don't you?

PIED. Oh, yes.

GOLDIE. Do you think Jason might like to go?

CINDERELLA. Jason?

PIED. Oh, no, he doesn't like to be around me. I attract cats and things.

GOLDIE. (*Sighing.*) Yes, I've noticed.

PIED. Well, ladies, shall we lead the parade? (*They approach door, take a deep breath, rush out.*)

MELBA. Well, now we can settle down to some good, deep gossip. I guess you heard about my old crony Sam Troll and that damn grouchy goat.

(*There is at this time a fierce commotion of the first order off stage. JASON and PRINCE enter carrying between them a small, wrinkled little man who is kicking, cursing, screaming, and wriggling.*)

JASON. We got him! We got him! It came to me like a bolt out of the blue! "A.E." it said. Inspiration. Like that!

CINDERELLA. "A.E." came to you? (*She looks at MELBA who shrugs.*)

JASON. I looked up everyone whose first names started with A or E and when we got to A.E. Rumplestilskin, here he was! We found our man!

(*They sit A.E. down. He looks around cringingly.*)

A.E. (*Whining.*) What is this? A plain, simple man in his own home, living his own life, enjoying the fruits of labor—

PRINCE. That means testing the product of his still.

A.E. And these hoodlums come and tear me away. (*Obsequiously.*) A poor old innocent man.

MELBA. A.E. Rumplestilskin—you old buzzard! You haven't changed a whit!

A.E. Who the dickens are you?

MELBA. A.E.! You don't remember!

PRINCE. Allow me to present Cinderella's godmother.

A.E. Godmother?

MELBA. Remember Melba? Junior Prom?

A.E. Oh. You. Well, you changed a lot. Life ain't been good to you, huh?

MELBA. Talk like a pig, be a pig! (*She stretches her arm, he cringes, they rush to stop her.*)

CINDERELLA. Melba, no! No! We need him!

PRINCE. Jason, some straw, the wheel—

A.E. What for? What's that for?

JASON. For you. To spin straw into gold.

A.E. Straw into gold?

JASON. Can't you spin straw into gold?

A.E. Only thing you can spin straw into is doormats. Course you got a lot of doors. (*He glances around at doors. A look of disappointment settles over the others.*)

MELBA. (*After a moment.*) I guess, if he can't spin straw into gold, we'd better just send him back to Euphoria to answer those attempted kidnapping charges.

A.E. What are you talking about? That wasn't kidnapping! She promised me that baby!

MELBA. What for?

A.E. For spinning straw into—

MELBA. Ah ha!

A.E. Well, that was different!

MELBA. What was different about it?

A.E. The king was stupider.

PRINCE. What's that supposed to mean?

MELBA. It doesn't matter! Just get started! Get the straw and let's see what he can do.

A.E. (*Grabbing his back.*) Oh! My back! My back! Oh! A chair! (JASON *gets him a chair, runs it into him.*) OW! You stupid— (A.E. *stands upright.*)

MELBA. I thought your back was giving you trouble.

A.E. (*Remembering, grabs back.*) Oh, my back! I can't work today.

MELBA. (*To* PRINCE.) Set him up.

A.E. My back—

MELBA. Is gonna really hurt in a minute! (A.E. *gives her a dirty look.*)

JASON. Straw and a wheel, right?

A.E. Well—

JASON. What else do you need?

A.E. I'm just a poor harmless old fellow. What harm have I ever done anyone?

JASON. What else do you need?

A.E. It's kind of hard to work on an empty stomach. (*They look at each other.*)

CINDERELLA. There's some fresh eggs and ham in the kitchen.

A.E. Eggs?

CINDERELLA. What did you have in mind?

A.E. I work real well on champagne.

PRINCE. Champagne?

A.E. Like oiling a fine machine, you know. (PRINCE *nods to* JASON, *who crosses to buffet.*)

JASON. Champagne coming up.

PRINCE. What else?

A.E. (*Fawningly.*) Well, now your majesty—sir— it's just—these are talents it's taken me a lifetime to develop. (*Pause.*) An old man like me, he's got to use the few talents he's got to prepare for his old age.

(*At the buffet table the champagne explodes, foam and liquid flying everywhere,* JASON *trying apol-*

*ogetically to stop the flood and to clean up what
he has done.*)

PRINCE. Continue.

A.E. Well, it's just that if I use my talents to make
gold for just everyone who asks me, without any reward—you see—

PRINCE. We shall see that you are handsomely re-
warded.

A.E. Well, now, not that I don't trust your Majesty, you being a good king and all— (*To* JASON
bringing champagne.) Thank you, son. Shame about
your arm, son. As I was saying, your Majesty, a good
business deal is always concluded first, you know?

MELBA. If you will spin straw into gold for us, I
will personally not turn you into a three-headed toad!

A.E. That— That's a bargain, all right.

PRINCE. I think you will find we can be more than
generous.

MELBA. As generous as the emperor of Euphoria,
certainly.

CINDERELLA. Extortion just comes naturally to you,
doesn't it?

MELBA. We all have our talents.

PRINCE. Is there anything else you need? If not,
let's get started and—

A.E. Oh, but there is!

MELBA. What?

A.E. Uh—water.

JASON. Water.

A.E. And—an oven.

JASON. An oven?

A.E. Gotta bake it, you know.

JASON. There was nothing said about baking in the
rumors I heard.

A.E. It's my new process, boy.

PRINCE. Well, let's all go to the kitchen.

A.E. Oh, no!

MELBA. What do you mean, no?

A.E. Nobody sees my secret process. Trade espionage everywhere. Can't trust anyone. Just take me to an oven and stand back.

PRINCE. With guards at the door, of course—to keep out spies.

A.E. Oh, yeah. Of course. (MELBA *takes one arm,* JASON *takes the other. They guide* A.E. *off stage.*)

CINDERELLA. You think it will work. (PRINCE *stands a moment, then slowly shakes his head negatively.* CINDERELLA *rushes to his arms.*) Oh, Charm.

PRINCE. If it doesn't work, I don't know what we'll do. I truly don't.

CINDERELLA. We'll manage. We've always managed.

PRINCE. I've got to get a job, Cindy.

CINDERELLA. You have a job. You run an empire.

PRINCE. I run it along a very rocky financial course.

CINDERELLA. But you run it.

PRINCE. What could I do? There's nothing I could do. I can't farm, can't makes shoes, can't bake pies, don't even know how to make war. I can't do anything. But I'll go down to the townsmen and ask what's open. What can I do?

CINDERELLA. (*Hesitantly.*) You can—speak well.

PRINCE. (*Astounded.*) Cindy!

CINDERELLA. (*Defensively.*) So what's so bad about giving royal tours of the kingdom? It's better than working for your subjects at something you know nothing about. You're the ruler. This is no ordinary world. This is the Enchanted Kingdom! You have a responsibility to memory and dreams, a responsibility for a world that lives beyond all pain.

PRINCE. I won't have it! I won't have hordes of foreigners pouring through here with cameras and tape recorders, stealing flowers and rocks and playing god awful radios—

CINDERELLA. Well, I will, and I'm the queen! (JA-
SON *rushes in*.)

JASON. Well, Your Majesty, Queen Cinderella, we've
got him started! Straw piled up, ovens on, spinning
wheels going—except for that one I broke—sorry
about that—now it's just a matter of time till the
gold rolls out. We'll be the financial leaders of the
world! Now that's a reason to have a royal ball! (*In
his joy he crashes into the coffee table, spilling it and
its contents all across the stage floor and knocking
the king and queen down.*)

CURTAIN

SCENE 2

TIME: *That evening.*

SCENE: *The royal ballroom. The coffee table has been
    removed. We hear Cole's Fiddlers Three with
    Pied on his flute. The lights fade up to reveal
    couples waltzing on this enchanted evening. The
    stage dims and a single spot hits center stage.
    The couples continue to waltz occasionally
    changing partners. Those speaking waltz or
    stroll into the spotlight and out after their lines.
    PRINCESS 1 and JACK CALDWELL enter the spot
    lighted area.*

PRINCESS 1. And I guess you heard about the Emperor of Glastonia?

JACK. No, I've been up the bean stalk all week.

PRINCESS 1. Well, it was positively scandalous. He
simply had nothing on. That's all.

JACK. But what about the beautiful clothes the
men made?

PRINCESS 1. There were none! That was the whole
point. It was a hoax and fraud from the beginning.

(*They dance out of the light*, PRINCESS 2 *and* PRIN-
     CESS 3 *stroll by*.)

PRINCESS 2. And he chose to marry the *eldest*
princess! After all the dancing they did for him and
all they looked after him, he chose her!

PRINCESS 3. It's unheard of! The prince always
chooses the youngest! Always! Choosing the eldest is
against the rules!

PRINCESS 2. Sometimes a prince chooses the middle princess.

PRINCESS 3. When? When does the prince ever
choose the middle princess? He always picks the
youngest!

PRINCESS 2. Sometimes he chooses the middle princess! (*They storm off*. JASON *and* RAPUNZEL *dance
in*.)

JASON. I'm really glad you got out of your tower,
Rapunzel, in time to come to the ball.

RAPUNZEL. Please, darling, you're on my hair!

JASON. (*Jumping aside*.) Oh, terribly sorry, Rapunzel. (*They dance out*. PRINCE *and* RED *dance in
with* RED *clinging very closely*.)

RED. I love dancing with you. You're such a
superior dancer. And so handsome.

PRINCE. Well, I always have danced well. Met
Cinderella at a dance, as a matter of fact.

RED. Oh, yes. Cinderella. Wasn't she a—scrub
woman?

PRINCE. Well, not exactly a—scrub woman.

RED. I've always felt a ruler should marry royalty.
I mean, it's terribly democratic of you to marry a
commoner.

PRINCE. Well, she's—she's—

RED. Did she know Melba then?

PRINCE. Of course. Melba is her godmother.

RED. Does Cinderella truly appreciate how fortu-
nate she is?

PRINCE. Well, she—uh—

RED. Do you know what I've never been able to understand?

PRINCE. What?

RED. Why she calls you Prince. I mean, you are the King, aren't you?

PRINCE. Well, uh—yes, yes, I am.

RED. If I lived here I would call you King Charming.

PRINCE. (*Embarrassed.*) Aww, Red—

RED. No, you are. The king of the charmers! A king must be terribly wealthy.

PRINCE. Do you think so?

RED. Especially now that A.E. is here. And Melba.

PRINCE. Melba? She doesn't bring money in!

RED. (*Looking into darkened area.*) Shhhh! Here she comes. Let's dance across the room.

(*They dance out as* MELBA *and* ALETTA *walk into view.*)

ALETTA. It is simply too much, you know. A cat living next door in such luxury. I cannot abide it.

MELBA. Have you ever thought of investing in motion pictures?

ALETTA. And he dresses like a cavalier, as though he were a human being.

MELBA. You can really rake it in with the right stars and script.

ALETTA. He has the audacity to wear little boots and a feather in his cap.

MELBA. Have you seen any of the Melba movies?

ALETTA. I say, are you listening?

MELBA. Uh, you said there was a cat living next door.

ALETTA. Well, don't you think that's terrible? Think what it does to the property value!

MELBA. I am trying to talk to you about movies.

(*They exit.* JASON *and* GOLDIE *enter. They say very little; they dance in each other's arms, very close.* GOLDIE *looks up and smiles.*)

JASON. You're lovely when you smile, you know that?

GOLDIE. Thank you, Jason.

JASON. You went walking with Pied today, didn't you?

GOLDIE. Yes, the Queen arranged it.

JASON. Pied Piper's the luckiest man in the kingdom, you know that?

GOLDIE. Oh, I don't know. It isn't very lucky to have flies following you all the time.

JASON. It is if *you're* with him. Why, I wouldn't even mind the cats, if you were with me.

GOLDIE. Cats?

JASON. They get my arm, you know.

GOLDIE. Oh. I'm sorry about your arm.

JASON. Oh, I don't mind. I'm adjusted to it now. I understand no girl could ever—well, I know how odd I look. No girl could ever, seriously—

GOLDIE. Oh, Jason, that's untrue! (*She gently pets his swan arm.*)

JASON. Goldie—

GOLDIE. Oh, Jason—

JASON. If I had two arms right now—

GOLDIE. You have one. (*They look deeply into one another's eyes, then he pulls her close to him. Before he kisses her, however, she screams.*) Jason, you're on my toes!

JASON. Oh, sorry. I'm sorry, Goldie.

GOLDIE. It's all right.

JASON. Is it truly, my dear?

GOLDIE. Jason, your feathers are caught in my ring!

JASON. Oh, terribly sorry. I'm really sorry, Goldie.

GOLDIE. Oh, Jason, there's no one like you in the whole world. No one. You are so dear.

JASON. Aw, well, gee, Goldie—

(*They waltz out in an embrace.* RED *and* MELBA *pause before the crowd, drinking punch.*)

RED. Oh, Melba, I'm so glad I caught you. I wanted to talk to you about the gold spinner. Fascinating, isn't it?

MELBA. I never thought A.E. Rumplestilskin was fascinating in my life.

RED. I wasn't referring to A.E.

MELBA. Oh?

RED. No, I was referring to the fact that an old fake like him could suddenly spin straw into gold. It's almost like he had some help, isn't it? Some magic help.

MELBA. However he does it, I'm sure it will be a help to the Kingdom.

RED. I really think it's all terribly interesting. I think the Godmother Council will be vitally curious about all this, don't you think.

MELBA. Certainly not. Miracles are a dime a dozen to them.

RED. I'll bet they'll be fascinated. I'll bet they'll reward someone handsomely for pointing it out to them.

MELBA. I wouldn't think of bothering them with something as petty as this.

RED. I think they'll pay through the nose to hear how a straw spinner in the castle of your god daughter was miraculously able quite out of the blue to make pure gold.

MELBA. Personally, I think they'll be bored stiff.

RED. Of course, if the reward they might offer were equalled by someone equally interested in the information—

MELBA. Oh, yes. I see.

RED. The thing is, the Council is so apt to reward

one with gingerbread houses and seven league boots. I want gold. Pure, shining gold. That's easy enough to understand, isn't it?

MELBA. Oh, sure. I never cared much for gingerbread myself.

RED. I'm so glad we understand each other. (RED *tips her glass to* MELBA, *crosses to punch bowl.* MELBA *sneers at her, exits in opposite direction.* CINDERELLA *and* PRINCE *enter dancing.*)

CINDERELLA. I just can't help but feel that you've been much too attentive and—

PRINCE. Why, Cinderella! I do believe you're jealous!

CINDERELLA. I am not! I just feel that a man your age—

PRINCE. My age?

CINDERELLA. Yes, your age. You are getting on, you know. And out. (*She pats his tummy.*)

PRINCE. Yes, and I suppose you're wearing your little glass slippers this evening.

CINDERELLA. Nobody's feet stay the same size through five pregnancies!

PRINCE. Ah! I've touched a sorepoint!

CINDERELLA. Listen, Prince Charming—

PRINCE. Why do you always call me "Prince"?

CINDERELLA. (*Taken aback.*) What?

PRINCE. Junior's the Prince. I'm the King.

CINDERELLA. Well—well— (*They dance out.* ALETTA *and* NANINE *walk by.*)

ALETTA. I mean, he can claim all he wants "a fairy" gave Pinocchio to him. Fairies don't give you babies. You know what I mean?

NANINE. Turned his puppet, a wooden puppet, into a live boy. Wow! I don't know how he thought that could make it around.

ALETTA. Well, the resemblance alone gives it away. Those long noses. Wonder what happened to the mother. (PIED *interrupts them.*)

PIED. Excuse me, have you seen Miss Goldilocks? (*They shake heads no.*) I haven't seen her since the beginning of the evening. I wonder where she could be. (*They move on. We hear him continue his questioning.*) Have you seen Goldie? (PRINCE *and* RED *dance in.*)

PRINCE. I'm afraid you have some misconceptions about this kingdom. I'd like to explain to you.

RED. Why, I'd love to hear more about this kingdom. Especially from the king himself.

PRINCE. It's about the finances.

RED. My favorite subject! Why don't we go outside where it's more—private. We can be alone there. (*As they exit we hear her last line.*) Does Melba have access to your treasury?

(CINDERELLA *moves into the light and watches them leave. She is joined by* GRETCHEN.)

GRETCHEN. Oh, Cinderella, I'm just so thrilled to be here at the Royal Ball. It's been a wonderful evening.

CINDERELLA. Thank you.

GRETCHEN. I'm just so sorry Mama couldn't come. But she's locked herself in the fallout shelter and won't come out for anything. She's convinced the sky is falling. Someone told her that.

CINDERELLA. Oh, yes. That midget chicken. It's nothing to worry about. Happens every fall.

GRETCHEN. I guess about everybody else in the world is here, don't you?

CINDERELLA. (*Glancing up toward a darkened platform, stage right.*) Not everyone. Excuse me, will you. (*Music and dancing continue, dimly lit, but spot fades. A light comes up on a tiny raised platform, full of straw and* A.E. *He is busily working, although we can't see his results.* CINDERELLA *slowly draws near his workroom and stealthily peers in. At this moment*

*we hear a loud feminine scream followed by a splash.
A.E.'s light fades, the light on the ballroom brightens.
The crowd rushes out to see what has happened.* CIN-
DERELLA *returns to the ballroom and meets* MELBA,
casually walking against the stream of the crowd.
MELBA *and* CINDERELLA *are alone on stage. Music has
stopped.*) What happened?

MELBA. Oh, some poor girl fell in the moat.

CINDERELLA. Good heavens! Aren't you going to
help?

MELBA. She'll be saved, I'm sure. (CINDERELLA
starts to rush out, then turns.)

CINDERELLA. You didn't mention the girl's name.
How does—ah—Red Riding Hood strike you?

MELBA. (*Helping herself to punch.*) I do believe
that was her name, poor child. Punch?

CINDERELLA. Yes, thank you. How did this unfortunate accident occur?

MELBA. I believe the poor girl was getting too near
something and lost her balance.

CINDERELLA. Getting too near what?

MELBA. The truth. (*She lifts punch cup to toast.*)

CINDERELLA. Oh, Melba!

MELBA. She'll be all right. Just a little warning. So
how's A.E.? Checked his progress lately?

CINDERELLA. (*Hesitantly.*) I was just looking in on
him.

MELBA. Well, he says it's a slow process. Wouldn't
let me see how he does it. But he'd better do it right!
I've come upon an unexpected problem and may need
a little extra cash. Surely within a couple of weeks,
with my help, he'll have enough to back my movie.

CINDERELLA. No.

MELBA. What do you mean, no?

CINDERELLA. I mean no.

MELBA. Cindy—

CINDERELLA. What tiny bit of money we can gather
is for Prince—King Charming. He needs it.

MELBA. I need it!

CINDERELLA. No, you don't! Charm is so worried about money he's desperate. He wasn't that way before I came into his life and the difference, Melba, is you!

MELBA. I'm not all of it.

CINDERELLA. You're most of it! We could make enough money to survive if it weren't for your exorbitant demands! Charming is a fine man and a good king. There's love and warmth and freedom in this country—and happy endings, Melba! Because of Charm and his family. And I won't let you destroy him anymore. It's humiliating for a man from a line like that to have to go before his people and look for work. His work is running this kingdom!

MELBA. You're breaking my heart.

CINDERELLA. Melba, I warn you—

MELBA. And I warn you, buck teeth! Callous knuckles!

CINDERELLA. I don't care what you say!

MELBA. I need that money to back my artistic work. That's my soul, my spirit! A masterpiece is waiting inside me!

CINDERELLA. There's nothing waiting inside you! Nothing! You've failed movie after movie after movie because the movies were no good! You have no talent for movies! You can do a lot of things, Melba, a lot of things. But you can't make good movies! They are everything the critics say. They're rotten! And no more Enchanted Kingdom money is going to back them!

(MELBA *stands in a rage. She breathes heavily. Then she lifts her arms dramatically and points.*)

MELBA.
Gods of the thunder!
Gods of the storm!

Guardian forces!
Cinders still warm!

Pumpkins and lizards,
Gods of the ball!
Hear me, Immortals!
Hear me all!
    CINDERELLA. (*Terrified.*) Melba! No!
    MELBA.
See into this daughter,
Unloving, unkind.
I call you to judge her!
See into her mind!

I implore your decision
By ingratitude's laws.
Make her again
The wretch that she was!

(*Smoke explodes from the ground,* CINDERELLA
    screams as the curtain drops.)

ACT III

TIME: *The following morning.*

SCENE: *The ballroom.* PRINCE *is pacing up and down, talking, it seems at first glance, to a locked closet.*

PRINCE. I don't know why you have to act like this! I didn't do anything but dance with that girl and if you must know the dress hobbled her so she wasn't even a good dancer! (*Pause.*) Cinderella! (*Pause.*) Cinderella, will you come out of that closet! Cindy, I'm asking you nicely. Come out!

CINDERELLA. (*Her conversation is heard from behind the door until she comes out late in the act.*) No!

PRINCE. I have never known you to be so unreasonable! You can't spend the rest of your life in that closet!

CINDERELLA. Yes, I can!

PRINCE. Cinderella! (*Silence.*) Ohhh!!! (*He paces.*) Jason! Jason! Melba! Where is everybody? (RED *enters, sneezing, carrying a tissue box with her.*)

RED. Good morning.

PRINCE. Have you seen Jason?

RED. Do.

PRINCE. Have you seen Melba?

RED. Do.

PRINCE. Well, what have you seen?

RED. The moat.

PRINCE. Oh. Listen, I'm really sorry about that, Red—

43

RED. Also the treasury.

PRINCE. The treasury?

RED. It's emdy.

PRINCE. I know.

RED. There's dothing id it.

PRINCE. After you fell in, I had it drained.

RED. I'm talking about the treasury. (*Sneezes.*)

PRINCE. Yes, well, that just drained away all by itself. (*Bangs on door.*) With some help!

RED. Was Melba some of that help?

PRINCE. Who knows where money goes? Or where it comes from?

RED. Maybe A.E. knows. I think I'll check on him.

PRINCE. I thought he didn't want anybody watching him.

RED. Well, I'm going to talk to him. Maybe I cad persuade him. (*Sneezes.*)

PRINCE. (*To door.*) You hear that? She's going to watch the gold being made! You're keeping us from watching too.

RED. (*Staring at him.*) Do you always talk to doors?

PRINCE. (*Embarrassed.*) Uh, no, not always. (*Kicks door.*)

RED. (*Exiting.*) Boy! And I thought the wolf was bad!

PRINCE. (*Shouting.*) Jason! Jason! Where are you? Melba! (MELBA *enters with a large bowl of pudding.*)

MELBA. You don't have to yell the house down!

PRINCE. Where have you been?

MELBA. What do you mean? I've been around, baby.

PRINCE. Well, where? I've been calling you!

MELBA. So what's your problem?

PRINCE. Cindy's locked herself in the closet and won't come out.

MELBA. Poor child.

PRINCE. Well, do you know anything about it?

MELBA. Maybe yes, maybe no.

PRINCE. What's that supposed to mean?

MELBA. Nothing, nothing at all. Perhaps she is embarrassed to face you.

PRINCE. Why would she be embarrassed to face me? That's the silliest thing I ever heard. What are you eating?

MELBA. Plum pudding.

PRINCE. Oh, really? I knew a kid at Prince School, stuck his thumb in his pudding, pulled out a plum, slicker'n that.

MELBA. Fascinating.

PRINCE. Did it 98 times in a row.

MELBA. Rich pudding. (*She knocks on closet door.*) How are you looking this morning, darling?

CINDERELLA. I'm gonna kill you, Melba!

MELBA. Change your mind?

CINDERELLA. NO!!

PRINCE. What are you talking about? Are you responsible for her being in there, you old biddy? (MELBA *turns angrily, aims her arm.*) I didn't mean it, Melba. Lovely Melba. Movie star Melba.

MELBA. Well . . .

PRINCE. I don't know how you've missed the Oscar all these years.

MELBA. (*To closet.*) Some people think I have no talent!

PRINCE. Oh, Melba, you have lots of talent. I don't know another living soul who can turn a king into a lizard like you can. (*Shudders.*)

MELBA. Child's play! I need something more challenging. Like the movies. You make magic with the whole world instead of some little numb-skull ruler. You make people believe the good guy always wins and love brings happiness and garbage like that. Now that's real magic!

PRINCE. Yeah, I guess it is. Have you seen Jason this morning?

MELBA. Not a feather. Haven't seen him since the

dance for that matter. (GOLDIE *and* JASON *enter holding hands.*)

GOLDIE. I have. (*She extends her hand.*) Jason and I were married last night.

(CINDERELLA *opens the door, stares out momentarily, mutters her line, then slams door again.*)

CINDERELLA. What?

PRINCE. Cindy—

JASON. Well, congratulate me!

PRINCE. Congratulations, Jason. (*He extends his hand to shake, meets with a wing, tries other hand, then just waves the whole thing off.*)

MELBA. Yes, congratulations, I'm sure. Lovely gold band.

GOLDIE. (*Looking at ring.*) Thank you.

MELBA. (*Posing to zot.*) Want a diamond?

GOLDIE. (*Jerking back.*) No! I like this!

MELBA. (*Shrugging.*) Suit yourself. (*After a moment.*) Want to look like him? (GOLDIE *gasps, grabs her arms,* JASON *jumps in front of her.*)

JASON. No, she doesn't, no, she doesn't! She loves me, but she doesn't want to look like me!

CINDERELLA. But your children!

GOLDIE. His genes weren't enchanted. (*To* JASON.) Were they?

JASON. I don't know. I never had any kids before.

MELBA. Well, we'll see.

GOLDIE. (*Half-heartedly.*) Yeah.

MELBA. You could start a whole new trend in the human race. It's not everyone who can do that. Be sure and invite me to the first child's christening.

GOLDIE. Oh, we will.

MELBA. (*Threateningly.*) Don't forget!

CINDERELLA. You leave that baby alone!

GOLDIE. Why is Aunt Cindy in the closet?

PRINCE. The girl has asked you a question, Cinderella. Why are you in the closet?

CINDERELLA. I like it here.

GOLDIE. I don't understand.

PRINCE. Neither do I.

GOLDIE. I'm going to tell Red about the wedding. Do you know where she is?

MELBA. I understand she's sick in bed with a terrible cold.

PRINCE. No, she's checking on A.E.

MELBA. (*Alarmed.*) On A.E.? What for?

PRINCE. She loves gold. Who knows what for?

GOLDIE. Be right back. (*Exits.*)

PRINCE. (*Kicking door.*) Cinderella!

CINDERELLA. Go away!

PRINCE. (*To* JASON.) See what you've gotten yourself in for? I should have known. The first time I saw her, she ran away from me. I should have known then it was her pattern of behavior. Find escape in flight. Never face reality. Run away. Hide in a closet. (*To closet.*) It's a form of paranoia, that's what!

MELBA. Schizophrenia.

PRINCE. Yeah.

MELBA. Avoidant schizophrenia.

PRINCE. Yeah! You hear?

CINDERELLA. No! I can't hear a thing. My ears are stopped up with cinders!

MELBA. Oh, please! No melodrama.

PRINCE. Ohhh! (*In disgust, the* PRINCE *sits in a chair left from the previous evening.*)

JASON. Shall I get you some coffee, sir?

PRINCE. Yes. (JASON *crosses to coffee on buffet.*) You think you know someone. You live with a woman twenty years, then one day she locks herself in the closet and won't come out.

JASON. (*Approaching* PRINCE.) Coffee, sir.

PRINCE. Careful, Jason. (JASON *tremblingly hands cup of coffee to* PRINCE. *It juggles, shakes, leans and*

drips, but does not spill. All breathe a sigh of relief.
JASON *beams.* PRINCE *holds the cup proudly. As* JASON
*turns to go, his wing hits the cup and spills it all
over the* PRINCE.) AHHHHHHHHH!!!!

CINDERELLA. (*Opens door.*) What happened? Oh.
Jason. (*Slams door.*)

JASON. Terribly sorry, sir.

PRINCE. I think we all ought to go separately and
implore the gods for Goldie's safety.

JASON. Sir—

PRINCE. Don't come too close, Jason.

JASON. No, sir.

PRINCE. What is it?

JASON. I just wanted to say that I think your decision—sorry about the coffee, sir.

PRINCE. It's all right, Jason.

JASON. I just wanted to say I think you were very
wise in reconsidering your decision about the tourists.

PRINCE. What?

JASON. I—I think it was very wise of you to allow
the tourists—

PRINCE. What are you talking about?????

JASON. The directive on my desk this morning.

PRINCE. On your desk?

JASON. When Goldie and I came in—

PRINCE. Saying tourists could come in here?

JASON. Well, selected tourists—

PRINCE. Selected tourists—

JASON. Yes, your majesty. (*There is an ominous
silence as* PRINCE *approaches closet.*)

PRINCE. Cin—der—ell-a! (*Silence.*) Cinderella, answer me! I demand that you answer me!

CINDERELLA. I never obey demands. You know that.

PRINCE. Did you authorize visitors in this kingdom?

CINDERELLA. I don't want to talk about it.

PRINCE. Cinderella!! (*He bangs on the door, stalks
around, glares at* JASON.) Have you already let some
in?

JASON. Just a few, sir.

PRINCE. Aghhhh! (*He storms to the windows and looks out.* GOLDIE *enters.*)

GOLDIE. Hi.

MELBA and JASON. Shhh!

GOLDIE. What's wrong?

PRINCE. (*Furious.*) What's wrong?! What's wrong!?

GOLDIE. (*Hesitantly.*) Yes, sir.

PRINCE. (*Inarticulate by now.*) Well! Well! Yes, and that! Well! Well! That's what's wrong!

GOLDIE. Oh.

JASON. Of course.

MELBA. We should have known instantly. (RED *enters carrying several gold bricks.*)

RED. Well, the gathered assemblage. (*She sneezes.*)

MELBA. What's the matter? Did you take someone seriously when they told you to go soak your head?

RED. Very funny, Melba.

GOLDIE. Oh, you brought some gold!

RED. Yes, isn't it interesting? (*She holds up a brick.*)

PRINCE. Interesting?

RED. Yes, I'd always heard before that A.E. was something of a shyster. I think the world will be so excited to hear of his success. I can hardly wait to spread the news.

MELBA. You could be persuaded to wait, of course.

RED. I guess it would depend on what else was occupying my mind at the time, don't you?

MELBA. It's so easy to get distracted these days.

RED. It's not easy for me to get distracted from long, shining, heavy bars of pure gold.

JASON. Oh, are they heavy? Here, I'll carry them for you.

(JASON *takes the gold bricks, but as he does so, he drops them. One strikes* MELBA'S *toe. She screams,*

draws back to zot, but restrains herself. The other
brick breaks.)

GOLDIE. Why, it broke.

JASON. Broke?

RED. Broke?

MELBA. Gold?

PRINCE. Let me see that. (*He picks it up. They*
gather around.) This is not gold.

JASON. It's fake!

MELBA. (*Complacently.*) A.E. always was a fraud
and a shyster.

JASON. It's just gold paint over straw bricks.

RED. (*In total disbelief.*) It's straw! It's straw!

MELBA. Same weave he uses for doormats. I wonder
how interested the Council will be in that?

RED. You never even had the power to help him!
You never did, did you?

PRINCE. What are you talking about? (*To* MELBA.)
What is she talking about?

RED. Doormats! I'm talking about doormats! (*She*
kicks a brick across the floor.) There! You'll have
guests with the cleanest shoes in the kingdom! Doormats for every door! (*She storms out.*)

GOLDIE. You'll have to forgive her. She was terribly
frightened by a wolf once and she has never been the
same.

MELBA. She probably saw it in a mirror!

PRINCE. (*Suddenly a plan occurs to him.*) Well, let's
go throw A.E. out! Get the guard! Let's do it! (*He*
gestures for them to go, but he himself ducks behind
the closet door.) Yes, sir, let's go down and see what
old A.E. has to say about this!

JASON. Yes, sir, and it's a lucky thing for the treasury that we have those tourists. (PRINCE *cannot*
reply, but shakes his fist. MELBA, GOLDIE *and* JASON
exit. The room remains in silence. Slowly the door
opens creakingly. CINDERELLA *peeks out, sees seem-*

ingly empty room, cautiously creeps out. PRINCE *grabs her. She screams, covers her face with her hands.*)

PRINCE. Ah ha! Caught you! Now will you explain this nonsense? (CINDERELLA *shakes her head negatively.*) Well, why not? I can't underst—Cindy, would you take your hands down? (*Again she shakes her head negatively.*) Cindy! Cindy! (*He forces her hands down. She wails. He is bewildered.*) What are you wailing about?

CINDERELLA. The way I look!

PRINCE. The way you look?

CINDERELLA. Yesss!!! (*She wails again.*)

PRINCE. You look like anybody looks the morning after. I've seen you worse.

CINDERELLA. What?

PRINCE. Well, you're no seventeen-year-old, but time hasn't been so bad to you.

CINDERELLA. Wha—what— (*She rushes to the enchanted mirror, looks in it, squinches nose, looks at teeth, wrinkles forehead, makes faces and incomprehendible sounds occasionally, indicating a rare form of joy. Calls out.*) Melba! Melba! (MELBA *re-enters, walks slowly over to her.*)

MELBA. Damn! I can't believe it!

CINDERELLA. Melba—

MELBA. I've never failed before!

CINDERELLA. What does it mean?

PRINCE. What's this all about?

MELBA. It means you've grown into it. You've grown into your beauty. It comes from the inside.

CINDERELLA. And you have no power over that, have you?

MELBA. Curses! (*She storms about, uttering various epithets; she kicks things. One is reminded of the stories rumored about Rumplestilskin throwing a fit through the floor.* CINDERELLA *laughs gleefully, hugs* PRINCE. MELBA *suddenly becomes obsequious.*) Cinderella—dear Cinderella, my darling god daughter.

You aren't going to forget your old godmother now, are you, girl? The old godmother who helped you so much when you needed help. I'll dedicate my next picture to you.

CINDERELLA. (*Every inch the beautiful Queen she has grown to be.*) I will not forget you, Melba. I always loved you. (*She hugs her.*) Now go and let me talk with my husband.

MELBA. *Pumpkin Trek*, it's called. About the people in this pumpkin-shaped spaceship and the things that happen to them on their five year mission to explore new worlds. Gonna net a cool million . . . (*She exits.*)

PRINCE. Would you tell me what's going on?

CINDERELLA. Never. But I will tell you one thing. I love you. Good enough?

PRINCE. Yes. (*They are about to kiss, but he pulls away.*) No! What do you mean authorizing foreigners to come in here?

CINDERELLA. Well, Charm—

PRINCE. No "well, Charm." I want a straight answer.

CINDERELLA. I went to see A.E. last night. I saw the bricks were false. I knew you'd never allow tourists, so I did it for you. It's the only way.

PRINCE. Hordes of people—

CINDERELLA. No hordes! Only five.

PRINCE. Five?

CINDERELLA. Or—ten, fifteen—

PRINCE. (*At window.*) Look at that one. Look at him. Just standing there staring at the new swan.

CINDERELLA. But they have to meet special qualifications before we allow them in.

PRINCE. What qualifications? Look at those. One's talking, the other's writing down everything that's being said.

CINDERELLA. We get a royalty from anything they write about us, Charm.

PRINCE. There's one talking with Pied! (*Changes*

voice.) Good heavens! There's Red walking with Midas! He's too young for her!

CINDERELLA. (*Teasing*.) She could be your daughter-in-law.

PRINCE. (*Astounded*.) She could not! (*Upset*.) Now one of those men is talking with them! Heathens! All over the kingdom!

CINDERELLA. They are not heathens! That's one of the qualifications.

PRINCE. So what are their qualifications? What do they have to be? Rich?

CINDERELLA. Not rich—

PRINCE. Just because some guy's born with money, he comes in here and queries my son about all his psychotic tendencies—just because he's rich—

CINDERELLA. Sensitive. Not rich. That's a qualification—sensitivity. Imagination. Creativity. These people must be full of humor and love. They must know pain and suffering. They must walk through gloomy caverns and haunted mines. They must be stoned and kicked and ridiculed and bruised, and they still must race toward life as an adventure. Most of all, they must carry hearts beating with the great overwhelming joy of childhood. They must believe in laughter. Only such mortals as these can ever be admitted to the Enchanted Kingdom, Charm. No others.

PRINCE. Are there such mortals?

CINDERELLA. Yes. These are writers, Charm, and artists. They'll give us a percentage of their works. A royalty. We'll never be without income again. And far away, mortals will hear of our world in the midst of their strife, in the midst of debt and pain and failure, they will hear of our kingdom and take heart.

PRINCE. Who are these visitors? (*They look out window*.)

CINDERELLA. The man by the swan lake is a Mr. Anderson—Hans Christian Anderson. The two men there are brothers. Grimm is their name. That's a Mr. Robert Browning there with Pied. Melba has helped us find them, I think, though she didn't admit it. She really cares for us, Charm. She'll send us others of the same special strain. There's a man from America, Charm, who wants to make a movie here.

PRINCE. Cameras! Microphones! Big Brother!

CINDERELLA. No! No cameras! It will all be drawn by Mr. Disney and his staff. He just wants to visit for a while. (*Pause.*) Look out there, Charm. There's no destruction, no violation of our dreams. Do you see that the kingdom is being hurt?

PRINCE. (*Looking out.*) Well, I guess not.

CINDERELLA. (*Puts arm around him.*) Oh, Charm, do you mind so much? The visitors are very special. (*Pause.*) Is it all right, Charm? (PRINCE *hesitates a moment, then draws* CINDERELLA *into his arms.*)

PRINCE. I love you, Cinderella. (MELBA *and* JASON *rush in.*)

MELBA. I've got it! I've got it! What we need is an entertainment center! Rides, a big hotel, restaurants, theatres—showing Melba movies exclusively, of course. Right, Jason? (JASON, *in his exuberance, knocks over a table.*) Where shall we put the theatre?

CINDERELLA. (*To* PRINCE.) You know what I think is the nicest thing about our relationship?

PRINCE. What's that?

CINDERELLA. Living happily ever after.

PRINCE. Only way to live.

MELBA. We'll put the Ferris wheel here, the underground tunnel there, conversations with the swan only a nickle—make that a quarter— We'll write Melba's Fun Center in bright neon over the gates of the Kingdom—gold and red lights flashing on and off—

(*Curtain*)

PROPERTY PLOT

ACT I:
    glitter, drops slowly onto scene
    alarm clock, on dressing table stage left
    hairbrush, on dressing table stage left
    Prince's clothes, on chair up right
    Cinderella's clothes, behind screen, up left
    pillows, on bed
    knick-knacks, on table up right
    curtains on window, down right
    letter, Jason
    quill, Jason carries in his arm
    magic wand, Melba
    lasso, Melba
    makeup and jewelry, dressing table stage left
    cowboy gun, Melba
    lamp, on table up right

ACT II:
    coffee pot and cups, table down center
    tarts, on buffet up left
    pie, on buffet up left
    champagne, on buffet up left

ACT III:
    kleenex, Red
    bowl of pudding, Melba
    coffee cups and pot, on buffet up left
    gold bricks, Red

ELECTRICAL PLOT

General lighting is used for Acts I and III and Scene 1 of Act II. In the ball scene, Act II, Scene 2, the overhead lighting is darkened. A spotlight hits center stage. Into this light the characters dance or walk to say their lines. A separate light is used to illuminate A.E. RUMPLESTIL-SKIN's platform, up right. It is visible in dim light when CINDERELLA visits him, is unseen the rest of the time.

ACT I:

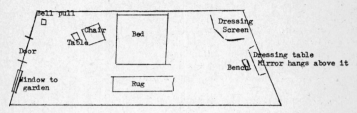

ACT II, SCENE 1:

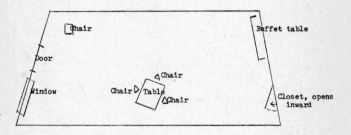

ACT II, SCENE 2:

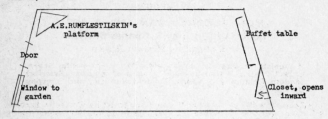

ACT III:

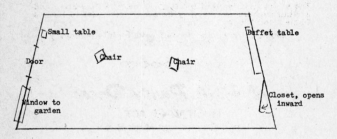

THE SENTIMENTAL SCARECROW

(ALL GROUPS)

MUSICAL-COMEDY-FANTASY—1 ACT
Book and Lyrics by S. Charles Shertzer
and Music by Nathan Brown

A musical version of Rachel Field's "The Sentimental Scarecrow." 2 men, 5 females, and a band of gypsies. (Exterior) Modern Costumes. 5 songs, incidental music, and a gypsy dance.

The Scarecrow is exactly what the title suggests; he wishes to become a human; in order to realize his wish, he must convince some young lady to not only kiss him, but to agree to marry him. The fun of this production is found in the Scarecrow's antics as he attempts to win a wife. The music and the lyrics are delightfully amusing, plus exciting, and at times filled with genuine pathos.

The songs include "Half the Day's Gone," "A Cold Stare and a Withering Glance," "Gypsy Caravan," "I've Got to Have a Dame," and "Funny Looking."

Music on rental and deposit, write for information.
Royalty, $15-$10.

◇◇◇◇◇◇◇

A Pink Party Dress

MUSICAL—1 ACT
David Rogers and Mark Bucci

A musical version of Margaret Bland's "Pink and Patches." 1 man, 3 females. (Exterior) Modern Costumes. 5 songs. 35 minutes.

The story of Texie, a mountain girl who hopes to escape the life of hardship and poverty her mother and other mountain women lead. She longs for the richer life she has observed at a fashionable hotel nearby and for a pink party dress instead of the patched brown denim she is forced to wear. Then a visitor to the hotel offers to give Texie a dress. Whether her proud mother will allow her to accept it and whether it will be the Pink Party Dress form the story of this charming folk musical.

The songs include "Women Folk Work Fer Men Folk," "A Pink Party Dress," "Lovely Evening, Isn't It?," and others. Complete libretto and piano score.

Royalty, $15.00 first performance
$10.00 each additional performance.

Musicals...

BEN FRANKLIN IN PARIS

CURLEY McDIMPLE • DAMES AT SEA

EL GRANDE DE COCA-COLA

FRANK MERRIWELL • GREASE

HOW NOW, DOW JONES • MAD SHOW

LAST SWEET DAYS OF ISAAC

MARVELOUS MISADVENTURES OF
SHERLOCK HOLMES

MINNIE'S BOYS • NOW!

PETER PAN • PURLIE • RAISIN

ROTHSCHILDS • SEESAW

TELEMACHUS, FRIEND • TRICKS

WHAT'S A NICE COUNTRY LIKE YOU
DOING IN A STATE LIKE THIS

ZORBA • VAGABOND KING

Information on Request

SAMUEL FRENCH, Inc.

25 West 45th St.   7623 Sunset Blvd.
NEW YORK 10036   HOLLYWOOD 90046

#1

6 RMS RIV VU
BOB RANDALL

(Little Theatre) Comedy
4 Men, 4 Women, Interior

A vacant apartment with a river view is open for inspection by
prospective tenants, and among them are a man and a woman
who have never met before. They are the last to leave and,
when they get ready to depart, they find that the door is locked
and they are shut in. Since they are attractive young people,
they find each other interesting and the fact that both are happily married adds to their delight of mutual, yet obviously separate interests.

> ". . . a Broadway comedy of fun and class, as cheerful as a
> rising soufflé. A sprightly, happy comedy of charm and humor.
> Two people playing out a very vital game of love, an attractive
> fantasy with a precious tincture of truth to it."— *N.Y. Times.*
> ". . . perfectly charming entertainment, sexy, romantic and
> funny."—*Women's Wear Daily.*

Royalty, $50-$35

WHO KILLED SANTA CLAUS?
TERENCE FEELY

(All Groups) Thriller
6 Men, 2 Women, Interior

Barbara Love is a popular television 'auntie'. It is Christmas, and
a number of men connected with her are coming to a party.
Her secretary, Connie, is also there. Before they arrive she is
threatened by a disguised voice on her Ansaphone, and is sent
a grotesque 'murdered' doll in a coffin, wearing a dress resem-
bling one of her own. She calls the police, and a handsome
detective arrives. Shortly afterwards her guests follow. It becomes apparent that one of those guests is planning to kill her.
Or is it the strange young man who turns up unexpectedly,
claiming to belong to the publicity department, but unknown to
any of the others?

> ". . . is a thriller with heaps of suspense, surprises, and nattily
> clever turns and twists . . . Mr. Feeley is technically highly
> skilled in the artificial range of operations, and his dialogue is
> brilliantly effective."—The Stage. London.

Royalty, $50-$25

~~~~~~

THE SEA HORSE
EDWARD J. MOORE

(Little Theatre) Drama
1 Man, 1 Woman, Interior

It is a play that is, by turns, tender, ribald, funny and suspenseful. Audiences everywhere will take it to their hearts because it is touched with humanity and illuminates with glowing sympathy the complexities of a man-woman relationship. Set in a West Coast waterfront bar, the play is about Harry Bales, a seaman, who, when on shore leave, usually heads for "The Sea Horse," the bar run by Gertrude Blum, the heavy, unsentimental proprietor. Their relationship is purely physical and, as the play begins, they have never confided their private yearnings to each other. But this time Harry has returned with a dream: to buy a charter fishing boat and to have a son by Gertrude. She, in her turn, has made her life one of hard work, by day, and nocturnal love-making; she has encased her heart behind a facade of toughness, utterly devoid of sentimentality, because of a failed marriage. Irwin's play consists in the ritual of "dance" courtship by Harry of Gertrude, as these two outwardly abrasive characters fight, make up, fight again, spin dreams, deflate them, make love and reveal their long locked-up secrets.

"A burst of brilliance!"—*N.Y. Post.* "I was touched close to tears!"—*Village Voice.* "A must! An incredible love story. A beautiful play!"—*Newhouse Newspapers.* "A major new playwright!"—*Variety.*

ROYALTY, $50–$35

THE AU PAIR MAN
HUGH LEONARD

(Little Theatre) Comedy
1 Man, 1 Woman, Interior

The play concerns a rough Irish bill collector named Hartigan, who becomes a love slave and companion to an English lady named Elizabeth, who lives in a cluttered London town house, which looks more like a museum for a British Empire on which the sun has long set. Even the door bell chimes out the national anthem. Hartigan is immediately conscripted into her service in return for which she agrees to teach him how to be a gentleman rather after the fashion of a reverse Pygmalion. The play is a wild one, and is really the never-ending battle between England and Ireland. Produced to critical acclaim at Lincoln Center's Vivian Beaumont Theatre.

ROYALTY, $50–$35

~~~~~~

#3

A Breeze from The Gulf

MART CROWLEY

(Little Theatre) Drama

The author of "The Boys in the Band" takes us on a journey
back to a small Mississippi town to watch a 15-year-old boy suf-
fer through adolescence to adulthood and success as a writer. His
mother is a frilly southern doll who has nothing to fall back on
when her beauty fades. She develops headaches and other
physical problems, while the asthmatic son turns to dolls and
toys at an age when other boys are turning to sports. The
traveling father becomes withdrawn, takes to drink; and mother
takes to drugs to kill the pain of the remembrances of things
past. She eventually ends in an asylum, and the father in his
fumbling way tries to tell the son to live the life he must.

> "The boy is plunged into a world of suffering he didn't create.
> . . . One of the most electrifying plays I've seen in the past few
> years . . . Scenes boil and hiss . . . The dialogue goes straight
> to the heart." Reed, Sunday News.

Royalty, $50—$35

ECHOES

N. RICHARD NASH

(All Groups) Drama
2 Men, 1 Woman, Interior

A young man and woman build a low-keyed paradise of happiness within an asylum, only to have it shattered by the intru-
sion of the outside world. The two characters search, at times
agonizingly to determine the difference between illusion and
reality. The effort is lightened at times by moments of shared
love and "pretend" games, like decorating Christmas trees that
are not really there. The theme of love, vulnerable to the sur-
veillances of the asylum, and the ministrations of the psychia-
trist, (a non-speaking part) seems as fragile in the constrained
setting as it often is in the outside world.

> ". . . even with the tragic, sombre theme there is a note of hope
> and possible release and the situations presented specifically also
> have universal applications to give it strong effect . . . intellectual,
> but charged with emotion."—Reed.

Royalty, $50—$35

VERONICA'S ROOM

IRA LEVIN

(Little Theatre) Mystery

2 Men, 2 Women, Interior

VERONICA'S ROOM is, in the words of one reviewer, "a chew-up-your-finger-nails thriller-chiller" in which "reality and fantasy are entwined in a totally absorbing spider web of who's-doing-what-to-whom." The heroine of the play is 20-year-old Susan Kerner, a Boston University student who, while dining in a restaurant with Larry Eastwood, a young lawyer, is accosted by a charming elderly Irish couple, Maureen and John Mackey (played on Broadway by Eileen Heckart and Arthur Kennedy). These two are overwhelmed by Susan's almost identical resemblance to Veronica Brabissant, a long-dead daughter of the family for whom they work. Susan and Larry accompany the Mackeys to the Brabissant mansion to see a picture of Veronica, and there, in Veronica's room, which has been preserved as a shrine to her memory, Susan is induced to impersonate Veronica for a few minutes in order to solace the only surviving Brabissant, Veronica's addled sister who lives in the past and believes that Veronica is alive and angry with her. "Just say you're not angry with her," Mrs. Mackey instructs Susan. "It'll be such a blessin' for her!" But once Susan is dressed in Veronica's clothes, and Larry has been escorted downstairs by the Mackeys, Susan finds herself locked in the room and locked in the role of Veronica. Or is she really Veronica, in the year 1935, pretending to be an imaginary Susan?

> The play's twists and turns are, in the words of another critic, "like finding yourself trapped in someone else's nightmare," and "the climax is as jarring as it is surprising." "Neat and elegant thriller."—*Village Voice.*

ROYALTY, $50–$35

MY FAT FRIEND

CHARLES LAURENCE

(Little Theatre) Comedy

3 Men, 1 Woman, Interior

Vicky, who runs a bookshop in Hampstead, is a heavyweight. Inevitably she suffers, good-humouredly enough, the slings and arrows of the two characters who share the flat over the shop; a somewhat glum Scottish youth who works in an au pair capacity, and her lodger, a not-so-young homosexual. When a customer—a handsome bronzed man of thirty—seems attracted to her she resolves she will slim by hook or by crook. Aided by her two friends, hard exercise, diet and a graph, she manages to reduce to a stream-lined version of her former self—only to find that it was her rotundity that attracted the handsome book-buyer in the first place. When, on his return, he finds himself confronted by a sylph his disappointment is only too apparent. The newly slim Vicky is left alone once more, to be consoled (up to a point) by her effeminate lodger.

> "My fat Friend is abundant with laughs."—*Times Newsmagazine.* "If you want to laugh go."—*WCBS-TV.*

ROYALTY, $50–$35

PROMENADE, ALL!
DAVID V. ROBISON

(Little Theatre) Comedy
3 Men, 1 Woman, Interior

Four actors play four successive generations of the same family, as their business grows from manufacturing buttons to a conglomerate of international proportions (in the U.S. their perfume will be called Belle Nuit; but in Paris, Enchanted Evening). The Broadway cast included Richard Backus, Anne Jackson, Eli Wallach and Hume Cronyn. Miss Jackson performed as either mother or grandmother, as called for; and Cronyn and Wallach alternated as fathers and grandfathers; with Backus playing all the roles of youth. There are some excellent cameos to perform, such as the puritanical mother reading the Bible to her son without realizing the sexual innuendoes; or the 90-year-old patriarch who is agreeable to trying an experiment in sexology but is afraid of a heart attack.

"So likeable; jolly and splendidly performed."—*N.Y. Daily News.* "The author has the ability to write amusing lines, and there are many of them."—*N.Y. Post.* "Gives strong, lively actors a chance for some healthy exercise. And what a time they have at it!"—*CBS-TV.*

ROYALTY, $50–$35

ACCOMMODATIONS
NICK HALL

(Little Theatre) Comedy
2 Men, 2 Women, Interior

Lee Schallert, housewife, feeling she may be missing out on something, leaves her husband, Bob, and her suburban home and moves into a two-room Greenwich Village apartment with two roommates. One roommate, Pat, is an aspiring actress, never out of characters or costumes; but, through an agency mix up, the other roommate is a serious, young, graduate student—male. The ensuing complications make a hysterical evening.

"An amusing study of marital and human relations . . . a gem . . . It ranks as one of the funniest ever staged."—*Labor Herald.* "The audience at Limestone Valley Dinner Theater laughed at "Accommodations" until it hurt."—*News American.* "Superior theater, frivolous, perhaps, but nonetheless superior. It is light comedy at its best."—*The Sun, Baltimore.*

ROYALTY, $50–25